D1026441

THE
ART
OF
GETTING
EVEN

THE
ART
OF
GETTING
EVEN

THE
DO-IT-YOURSELF
JUSTICE MANUAL

Gary Brodsky

CASTLE

Introduction

There are thousands of reasons why you might feel that you deserve restitution from someone who has wronged you. No matter how hard you try, there is always some stupid idiot with a penchant for screwing with you. The enemy comes in all shapes and sizes. Some of them are purposely after you, some strike unintentionally through ignorance, and some are just plain careless. Others seem to go out of their way to come out on top, and will step on anyone they have to, to get there. Whatever the reason, here's your chance to fight back. The dirty deeds I have included in this book are just the beginning. There are thousands of ideas that are custom made for any situation. With a little imagination, and practice, you will rest comfortably knowing that you're not going to be the helpless victim anymore. Soon you will be a qualified practitioner of the art of getting even.

There is no worse feeling than to be treated contemptuously by a fellow human being, and where you're helpless to respond. There is, however, no better feeling than taking the time to perfect a fitting revenge, and to carry it out successfully. Perhaps you have tried all legal resources, you've tried to work things out personally, and professionally, with little or no results. Now is the time to get down to business, and plan a secretive revengeful scheme. Your enemy may be just one person, then again it may be a powerful corporate organization. It could even be a blithering sappy idiot. Whatever the origin of your misfortune, a well planned act of artful revenge can make you feel like a million bucks. When the unsuspecting victim falls into your custom-tailored trap, your load is lightened considerably, and you can go on with living your life.

Always be patient and clear-headed when getting even. Some acts of revenge take weeks to execute. Others take longer, and some can be done in less than a minute. There are revengsters who hit their victim with one incredibly mind-blowing revenge, while others savor the feeling and hit back at their enemy again and again and again, leaving the target just short of insanity.

I will suggest that you exercise caution, and that you detail your revenge tactics accordingly in relationship with the grievance. Mold the act to fit the situation. You don't want to be throwing M-80's onto the laps of old ladies, or harm innocent animals who have no choice when it comes to the company they must keep. As they say, let the punishment fit the crime. If someone has treated you like crap, it's time to start to collect some of your own, while you decide which clever way to use it.

A finely executed revenge can be as rewarding as any personal achievement. There comes a time when you have got to stop being passive when it comes to dealing with the seedy realities of humanity. Plan your strategy, deliver the blow, and feel better, knowing that you are well on your way to mastering the fine art of getting even.

Good luck, and good hunting.

Gary Brodsky

The Art of Getting Even

Often, a subtle revenge can be a rewarding one. If you want to get back at someone who hasn't been a total jerk, but you and he/she knows that you've been wronged, sit near this person, and make sure that he or she sees you reading this book. If the person tries to talk or get you to reveal what act of revenge, if any, you are planning to perform, turn away with a brief, knowing smile, and slowly flip through these pages. You'll leave the craphead in puzzles, wondering where and when you'll strike.

Ahm Gonna KILL Mahself

Call the suicide prevention number, for the area that your victim lives in. Disguise your voice, and give the victim's full name. It helps if his number is in the phone book, this way the authorities will be able to look it up in a few minutes. Threaten to kill yourself, unless you get to talk to a TV reporter. Then sob as you say, "I've got a gun to my baby's head." Hang up.

Air Conditioner Blitz

Take a nice loose dog stool and chuck it onto the ventilation panel on the outside of the victim's air conditioner. The smell inside will be unbearable, and will probably never be found. The place will stink for weeks.

If you can, go into the person's house or office often, and comment each time, about the horrible smell. This will make the person even more angry. If it's a restaurant, call the health department. After all, it's just not healthy to have a dining area that smells awfully, of excrement.

Airport Shanagins

Once I had the privilege of driving a guy I hated to the airport. Since security check points are strictly regulated, I was certain that my prank wouldn't go unnoticed. While I was helping the guy unload his luggage from my car, I slipped a handful of 9mm bullets into his jacket pocket, along with a photo of Yassar Arafat. When he went through the metal detector, the bullets set off the alarm, and they checked his pockets. My prank worked better than I had planned, as the security people detained the guy for eight hours of intensive questioning.

Anti-Bum Antict

If you are accosted daily by the same bum, week after week, always asking you for a hand out, try holding a fifty cent piece with a pair of tweezers, and heating it red hot with a lighter. Don't actually hand this heated coin to the stinking bum, throw it toward him, so that it rolls past him. He'll chase it, and pick it up, and the burn will be with him. Now most bums are just victims of circumstance, so only do this to ones who are real pests. Leave the other poor sods alone.

At His Age?

Here's a good one to do for quick revenge. Say that you go into a men's room in a restaurant or other public place, and there's somebody you don't like in there. Take a cup of water and hit him in the crotch with it. The guy will stay in there for six hours, until the water dries.

More Than One Way to Skin a Bank

Go to the deposit slip area of the bank that's done you wrong. Take out a slip and write, "This is a stick-up" on the back of it. "Put all of your money on the counter, and I won't kill you. Hit the alarm, and I'll blow your face off." Slyly slide the slip back into the stack, about ten slips back. Finish your business, and leave the bank.

Another good bank prank, is to ask to use the phone. Usually, the tellers send you to an empty desk. Pretend to make a short call, while looking under the desk. You'll most probably see the foot-pedal alarm button. Push it with your foot, and leave. I suggest that you move quickly, and that you wear a disguise. Good banking!

The Ballpoint Pen Capper

Take the cap off of your victim's ballpoint pen. Hold the cap so that it is upright like a drinking glass. Take an eyedropper, and half fill the pen cap with ink of a matching color. Then snap the cap back on and replace the pen to it's original position. The fool will pick it up and pull off the cap, which will in turn spill the ink onto the person's lap. The blame will fall on the manufacturer of the pen. No one will suspect you.

Bathroom Lockout

G.G. of southern California likes to get even with bars and restaurants that have done him wrong, by going into the restrooms and locking the doors from the inside. He locks them as he's leaving, and then picks a spot near the restroom, so that he can watch person after person try the door, only to return to their seats, frustrated. I've seen him do this in a crowded bar, at the peak of the daily drinking season, with incredible results. The first couple times, the folks will just try the door, then return to their seats. But after a while, they begin to wait outside the door, until a line forms. The last thing they try, is telling the management, who in turn goes and opens the door with a key. Here comes the clincher. While locking the door, G.G. jams a toothpick into the outer lock. The bathroom should stay locked for the evening.

Break a Leg

Take a jar or tube of petroleum jelly, and coat your enemy's shower floor with it. Sure this is nasty. But if the victim's actions toward you deem it necessary, go ahead and do it. You'll be glad that you did. As soon as the person turns on the water and steps into the shower—slip, bang, boom.

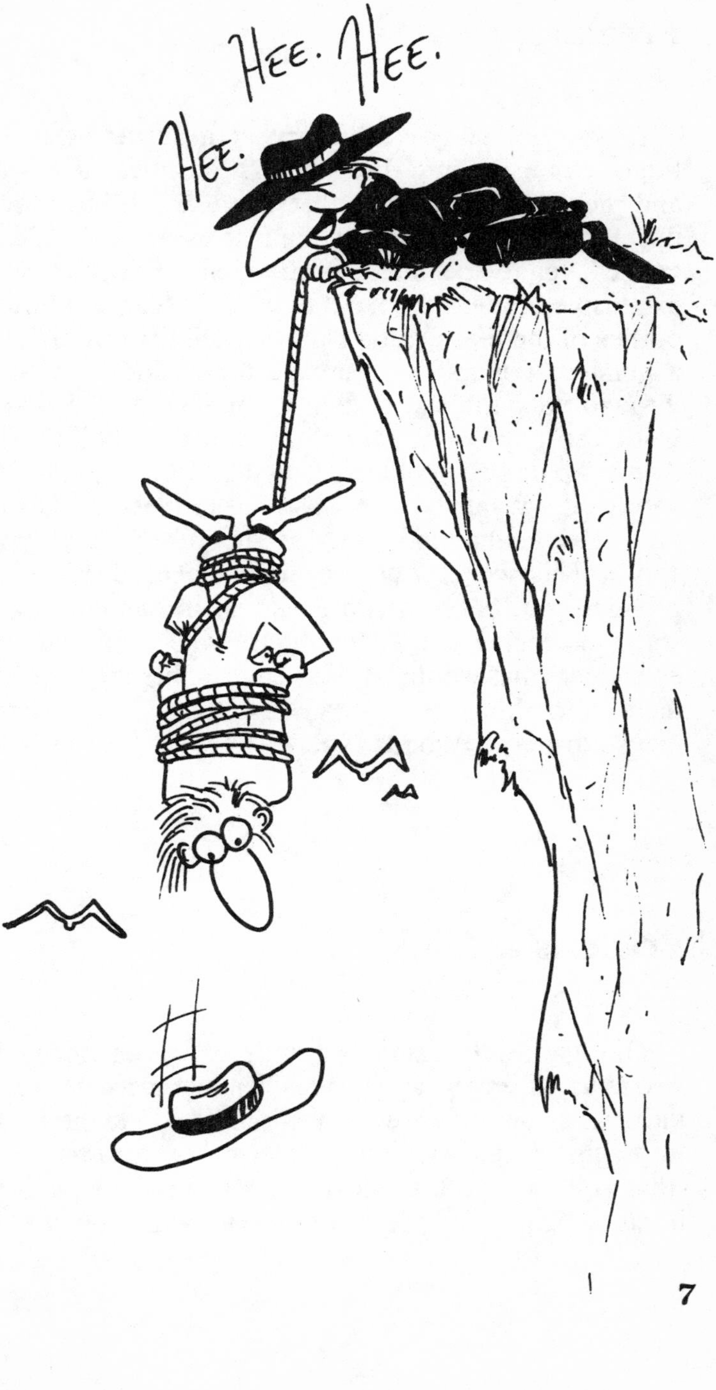
HEE. HEE. HEE.

Breaking Even

Let's say that you're angry at a supermarket or liquor store. Go into the store that has offended you, and pick up a few things that you want to buy. Pick up enough things, so that your arms are full. Then cruise over to the liquor section, and find the most expensive bottle of booze that the store carries. Some bottles of the really good stuff can sell for upwards of a hundred dollars. Pick up the bottle and let it slip through your fingers, so that it smashes on the floor. Until you pay for it, everything in a store belongs to them. Apologize profusely, saying, "Gee, I am SO sorry, all I wanted to do was read the label." Go to the check stand and pay for the other items you chose. This works with the high stacked displays of products too, but most stores are smart enough to not stack expensive bottled products, where the clumsy consumer (that would be you) can fumble them. Still, there is nothing better than knocking over an immense display of goods, you feel great.

Brick As a Trick

The good old-fashioned redbrick goes through windows as easily as it did when our parents were kids. As an adult, however, you should add to the mere throwing of it. Try tying a person's business card (that you hate) to the brick, and write on the back of it, something like, "Get out of town, while you can."

Bumper Thumpers

One of my favorite tricks is to put bumper stickers on the rear fenders of a victim's car. If you put them on the bumper, the stickers will be fairly easy to remove. If they are applied directly to the paint, they last a long time. Always apply firmly to the painted surface, and use epoxy to ensure a tight seal. Some clever sayings you can use are "Homosexuals for younger lovers," "Viet Nam veterans are pussys," "White supremists for a cleaner America," etcetera.

Larry, the Walla Walla Worm Wrangler recently used a bumper thumper to antagonize a friend for driving a certain type of automobile. He drove three hundred miles to place a sticker that read, "My other car is a piece of shit too" on the guy's truck. Sometimes you have to change your method of operation when pranking somebody. The guy drove his truck for a few days before noticing the sticker, but after seeing it and thinking it over exclaimed, "I'll bet Larry did this, why that . . ." You can bet that the truck owner will be plotting his own revenge against the Walla Walla Worm Wrangler.

Business Card Alterations

One time I took this guy's business card, which read something like, "Nelson Upbumper (Protecting the guilty)—Product Manager." I took the card to a printer and had him reprint one hundred new cards. The newly designed cards now read, "Nelson Upbumper (I wish that had been the guy's real name!) —Jew."

Cable Company Combat

If your local cable company is rude and uncooperative, or if they continuously overcharge you, seek out their satellite dish, during important events (such as the Superbowl, World Series, the final night's showing of a lengthy miniseries, etc.) and throw handfuls of ball bearings into the dish at appropriate times. If it's a sportscast you're trying to interrupt, take along a portable radio, so you know when an important play is going on. The cable company will get hundreds of calls, and letters. If you don't want to get that close to the dish, you can use one of those repeating BB guns, and hit it from long distance.

You can also park your vehicle next to the dish, and use a sideband radio to interrupt any transmission.

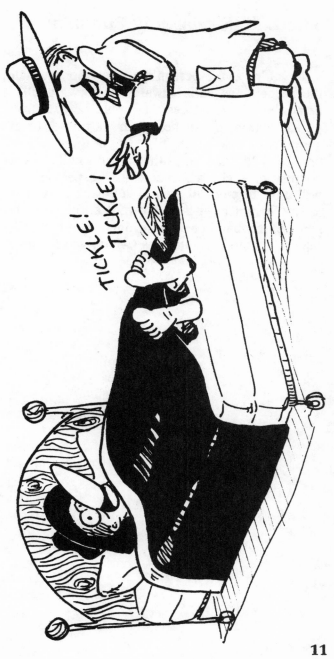

The Call Forwarding Clincher

If you're at the person's house who you hate, and the person has call forwarding, forward all of the person's calls to places that could be disastrous: the police station, his or her mother's house, or even to some exotic location like Egypt or Peru. If you choose to forward all of the victim's calls to a foreign country or such, whoever calls the person's number will have to pay full rates if someone answers.

Another method is to forward all calls to the person's ex-husband or ex-wife, including those pay-for-play telephone sex numbers (which you have set up.)

Camera Tricks

There are dozens of ways to get even with some-one with a camera, especially if the camera belongs to the person you're after. Take the victim's camera for a short amount of time, just long enough so that you can use it to your advantage, and then return it. One time this pest was over at my house, looking for a cigarette. Since this guy had bummed many a pack of my favorite smokes more than once, I decided to get even. He came with a camera, and had set it on the table. I told that I had a fresh pack of cigs, but that they were out in my car. I gave him the keys and told him to check in the glove compartment. The car was parked about a block up the street.

As soon as he left, I went to work. First I took a few close-up pictures of a nasty men's magazine, so that the pictures were all skin and blurry. I knew that his wife would see the shots, so my procedure be-came all the more satisfying. I held the camera be-tween my legs with my pants down. I photographed my behind, and my chest, leaving nothing to the imagination. Then I carefully put the camera back where my "friend" had left it. Soon enough, he re-turned with the smokes and then left. I found out later, that not only had his wife seen the pictures, but she and her mother had gone to pick up the photos, and they both looked at them over lunch.

Another way to do this, if you can't get a hold of the camera, is to use your own camera, take the same type of photos mentioned above, and take them to be developed where your victim usually takes his film to be processed. Fill out the appropriate information and drop the film off. The person will go to pick up his own film sooner or later, and think that he forgot about a roll that he had taken in, and pay for the developing.

Cameras are great. The new disposable 110 models are cheap and fit in a pocket. Keep one of these babies handy. You never know if you're going to see someone cheating on a friend, or getting too drunk. A photographic reminder keeps the enemy at bay, and you from getting any more guff from that person.

Those Camping Fools

Have you ever had a perfectly good camping trip ruined by Boom-box playing, loud partiers? Try mixing hamburger, honey, and a pint of sweet flavored schnapps, and smearing the loud bastard's car with it while they sleep. Don't just leave the stuff in a pile on the vehicle, rub it onto every portion of the car. The scent will surely attract bears or other forest creatures. The larger beasts, like bears, will climb all over the car, scratching the paint, and denting the top, hood, and body.

Another good one is to sling a rope tied to a fat pork chop or steak, over a tree limb over the sleeping camper's tent. The beasts will tromp all over the tent trying to get to the meaty treat, and hopefully, will step on a few faces in the process.

One time I was so mad at these outdoor partiers, that I swiped an outhouse from it's mounting, and dropped it off right next to the people's camp space. As soon as the sun came up, my friends and I each took turns using the outhouse, with the excrement, of course, just flopping onto the ground. Other campers saw the commode and used it too. By the time the jerks woke up and started cooking their breakfast, the booze began to churn in their stomachs. The stench was so unbearable, that my friends and I heard them puking, and their campsite smelled even worse.

Canned Food Foolery

With a razor blade or knife, remove the labels from canned food in your enemy's cupboards. Switch them with the labels from pet food. Switch tuna with cat food, beefy chunk dog food with canned stew, etc. Reglue the labels and replace them where you found them.

If your enemy owns a grocery store, buy the cans somewhere else (no need for the schmuck to make a cent of your money) and do the switcheroo, returning the doctored cans to his or her shelves. Be creative, be nasty, but best of all, get even.

Cash on Delivery

It may take you a little time, but order about fifty C.O.D. items, in your victim's name. The person will most certainly refuse to pay for the goods. That's fine. What you'll be doing though, is making the person have to deal with five to ten deliveries daily, that he or she is forced to refuse, that's a major hassle in itself. You'll also be getting the postal delivery person into a huff, from having to carry the packages to the person every day, only to return the stuff. This could lead to shoddy postal delivery or just a plain snotty attitude toward your victim. In other words, they're not going to be exactly friends after the fiftieth C.O.D. delivery.

Casual Cancellations

There are some utilities that you would have a very difficult time cancelling, like electricity, phone, gas, to name a few. The phone company makes sure of cancellations, by calling the person's home two to three times, to confirm the shut-off. They just won't do it unless they have confirmed the cancellation several times with the person.

There are services, however, which are not so strict and that are simply and quickly cancelled. Garbage pick-up, newspapers, diaper service, magazine subscriptions, water (bottled) delivery, etc. Find out what type of things your victim has, and devise your own custom shut-off scheme. As always, make the punishment fit the crime.

Car Door Locks

If you are able to get ahold of your victim's car keys, break them off in his door locks, after rolling up the windows tightly and locking all of the doors.

If you can't get the keys while remaining anonymous, use round toothpicks. Stick the toothpicks into the locks and break off any remaining portions. To insure a tight permanent fit, fill any gaps with the strongest bonding glue that you can find. Your revenge is delivered personally and sealed with a kiss.

Another method is to just ruin the lock on the driver's door, while leaving the passenger door lock untouched. This method enables the car owner to get into his vehicle and drive it, but only after climbing into the passenger side. The victim will undoubtedly be angry, but he probably won't call the locksmith right away, and you get to watch the phlegm-face struggle into his car every day. The gift that keeps on giving. Whether you ruin all the locks or only one, the result is time consuming and expensive for the car owner, and you'll feel a whole lot better.

Cassette Tapes

If you have access to your enemy's cassette collection, record over the music with your own choice of music. If the tapes are pre-recorded, simply cover the two small holes on the top of the cassette cartridge, and it'll be ready for you to go to work. If your enemy likes classical music, record over it with loud abrasive music, like Butt-hole Surfers, Kill Dozer, Beat Farmers, or any caustic music that you know will send the person screaming from his or her home. If the person likes the loud hard-core type of tunes, then replace it with Barry Manilow, Henry Mancini, or opera. Put the tapes back in the respective cases, and hit the road.

Cattle Calls

This one guy got me angry one too many times, (he was a real schmuckler) so I threw a cattle call at his office. A cattle call is used to acquire actors for movie or TV roles. Throw a cattle call in the local papers, for extras for a new movie. Ask for blacks, bikers, anyone who'll be really ticked off at your victim, and get basically irate. If the jerko lives in a metropolitan area, a few hundred "actors" should show up.

If the chump that you hate happens to be an actor, take out a classified ad in a newspaper you know he reads. Ask for someone who fits your enemy's description exactly—from color of hair, height, likes, dislikes, abilities, to the type of personality, etc. Make the ad too good to be true. Give the address of a local talent agency. At best, your acting "buddy" will be forced to see a few people who look just like him.

Cement Seat Covers

Science has developed some amazing new chemicals which provide an endless list of devious ways to get even. There is a product on the market, which comes in an aerosol can, which, when activated, releases a stream of quick drying foam. Some of these foams (which are used for house insulation or as a flotation filler for boats) unload the equivalent of fifty to one hundred pounds of cement when dry. They come with a handy little nozzle that you can pry into window cracks of cars, or into the engine compartment. Empty a whole can of this stuff under the hood of any car, and it'll render the motor useless. It might only take one or two cans to fill the entire passenger compartment of a mid-sized car. And it's permanent. These products can be purchased in most marine supply stores, or hardware stores. They are a great addition to the revengster's arsenal, and are fairly inexpensive.

Chainsaw Sex

Many toy stores carry a fun new gift item, the rubber chainsaw. They look real, and even have pull cords which sound almost like the real thing.

When your lover or mate suggests that the two of you engage in some perverted, kinky sex, (and you're not into it) pull the rubber chainsaw out from under the bed, and laugh deviously as you feverishly yank at the starting cord. You might want to add a few remarks like, "Quick! Do ten push-ups!" or "Grab your ankles!"

Change of Address

Go to the post office and take some of their change of address cards. Fill them out so that your victim's address is changed to a large metropolitan area. All of the person's mail will be forwarded there. Soon the person will notice a shortage of bills, letters, and even junk mail. By the time things get straightened out, much important mail will be lost, or obsolete.

Cigarettes

Carefully pour a little water into an open pack of your enemy's cigs. Just a few small dribbles renders the whole pack unsmokable.

If the bar or restaurant you're in is too smoky, don't complain. Help out. Buy a pack of your own, and light them one by one, until the whole pack is lit. Fill two ashtrays if you have to. The place will literally fill with smoke, and someone is sure to complain about you. When the bartender or waitress kindly asks that you extinguish your smokes, calmly mention how smoky the place was when you were trying to eat, and that you have as much right to smoke as much as you want, just as the other smokers had been doing.

Another way is to ask for a slice of cake or even a whole one. Stick your lit butts into the cake like birthday candles and ask that the waitress serve it to your "friend over there."

These tricks work whether you're a non-smoker or not. Say the maitre'd seats you in the smokers' section, way off in some abandoned corner of the restaurant. You're five miles from the kitchen, next to a solvent closet, waiting for service that never comes. Order the manager a piece of cigarette pie, or light up your whole pack. A whole pack of burning cigarettes in a restaurant, is like sending up a signal flare.

Ok, let's say that the person you want to get even with smokes. It doesn't matter if you do or not to enjoy this one. Tell the victim that you're an amateur magician, and that you want to show the person a fantastic trick. Ask for the person's pack of cigarettes, while promising that you won't damage the cigarettes. Ask the poor sucker to hold out both hands in front of him, like a double "stop" gesture. Carefully remove the smokes, a few at a time, and place them between his fingers. Be creative, put one in the victim's shirt pocket, in his mouth, above his ears. When the pack is completely empty, fein amnesia. Shake your head and say, "Shoot, I forgot how this trick works." Then crumple up the empty pack and walk away.

29

Classyfied Ads

Here's one I did to get back at a guy who really deserved it. I won't go into details, but he deserved what he got. This works best in Manhattan, because Manhattan real estate people would kill the victim. A lot of newspapers will take classified ads over the phone and bill you. So, you advertise apartments at unbelievable rates. Oh! This is great. You can also place one of those, "Must move. Selling everything cheap. Car, house, lawn furniture, household items," ads. Arrive early. Knock loud. The victim will go crazy when people start showing up around six AM, picking up and inspecting every little object around his house.

Commercial Bus Line Leeches

If you are as tired as I am with those idiots who insist on bothering you endlessly on long distance bus rides, try this. When you get off at your stop, and the schmidiot stays on, go into the bus station and approach the main desk. Tell the clerk that you just got off of bus number so and so, but that when you were riding, the guy who sat next to you kept mumbling about how he was going to kill the Governor. Say that he talked about it when you were listening and when you weren't. Give the clerk a fake name and address, and say that you'll cooperate in any way that you can to help, be it testimony or whatever. Leave a fake phone number, and tell the clerk to call you as soon as you get home. Now you can leave the station happy and relieved. Some folks really go out of their way to be a nuisance, so you have to go out of yours to get retribution. The talkative pest will probably never ride a bus again.

The Concealed Condom Caper

If your victim is married or living with someone, leave an empty condom wrapper near the bed or down the cushions of a couch or chair. Another way is to leave them on the back seat floor of the victim's car. Leave them anywhere that the victim's mate will find them. The mate will never believe the person's excuses, no matter what explanation the person comes up with.

If you want to, you can squirt some dish washing liquid into a rubber, and leave it somewhere. This is so gross, don't be surprised if the couple breaks up on the spot.

33

Credit No Credit

Find out the numbers of your intended victim's charge cards. You can either peek into the person's wallet or purse, or rummage through their garbage until you find bills or receipts bearing the numbers. Then call the companies that issued the cards, say that you're the card owner, and that they were all stolen. The next time the person tries to use the cards, all heck will break loose.

The Cutting Edge

Glass cutters are a cheap and easy tool for a quick revenge. Take the cutter and scratch lines into the glass of your victim's door glass, or window glass if it's near the door. Run the cutter along the wood or metal framing, so that the line cut is parallel to the frame. As soon as someone (not you of course) slams the door, the window will fall out.

Dead Animals

If you don't have any dead animals of your own, keep an eye out for fresh roadkills. Collect the damaged critters and put them in plastic bags. Freeze them for future use, or go ahead and use them fresh, if you can. You can wrap them up and send them to somebody, or you can simply toss them on his porch. If you feel like being really gross, you can take your dead raccoon, house cat, or whatever, and lay the corpse on the radiator fan of your victim's car engine. As soon as the car is started, the fan will act as an automotive blender (set on frappé) and it'll spread the animal's remains over the soon to be oven-hot engine. Mmmmm! Fresh cooked critters!

Deep Fried Revenge

Once, a friend of mine was tending bar at a cocktail lounge/restaurant, and a real plop-head was harrassing him about getting his appetizer. My friend went into the kitchen, and talked to the cook about what to do to get even with the insistant bugger. They decided against serving him the deep fried, battered zucchini that he'd ordered. Instead, they batter coated a bowl full of wine bottle corks, and deep fried them. The bartender served them up with a smile, and added that the appetizer was "compliments of the house." When the guy picked up the first cork, (the corks were cut in half the long way, and looked exactly like the real thing) and put it to his mouth, my friend almost burst out laughing. The guy took a bite, and you could almost see the recoil as his teeth sprung off of the deep fried treat. He tried again and again, finally realizing what was going on. My friend just stood there smiling at the guy, and looked him in the eye. He soon left, and hopefully, had a new understanding as he did.

The Diamond Studded Revenge

There is no more satisfying revenge tactic than the ruining of something expensive. I'm sure that you've heard the cliché saying, "Diamonds are a girl's best friend." Well, I have a new saying. "Zircon diamonds are a revengster's best friend." Zircon diamonds are very inexpensive, and they retain one quality of the real thing. Namely, they scratch glass just like diamonds. Buy as many of these beauties as you can, and make sure that they are the tiny kind. Take a handfull of these gems, and sprinkle them onto the windshield wipers of your enemy's car. Most newer automobiles have the wipers hidden for appearance sake, in a housing compartment just under the windshield. The victim won't see the tiny gems until the first rain, when the wipers are turned on. By then it is too late, and the windshield will be totally ruined. I like this one, because the car owner does the damage, all you do is offer him or her a gift. That just shows what a nice person you are, doesn't it?

Diesel Truck in a Can

One of my best quick acts of revenge is to scare the "doo-doo" out of people with one of those diesel horns in a can. I swear, if you're within twenty feet of someone, and you blast the air pressure activated horn, they usually lose their bowels on the spot. I like to blast them into bathrooms when someone stays in there too long, or point it toward lingering crosswalkers. There's nothing I hate more than some shithead dottying in front of my car when the walk signal is red, so I let loose with the horn out my window, and watch them jump to the sidewalk.

Well, the Dirty Bugger!

The victim who has children allows you a unique opportunity to revenge yourself. Call the child council board (there's one in every city) and the child abuse professionals under an assumed name. Tell them that you've witnessed foul acts of depravity between the victim and his or her children. Say that you've seen them beaten, and you can hear screams of terror late at night near the home. There will be a formal investigation into the lives of the victim and family. These investigations can be overwhelming to any adult, innocent or not. Be sure to make anonymous calls to the person's boss or neighbors, mentioning the horrible charges that were brought up by the child abuse prevention people.

Down It

Take a small- to medium-sized down-filled pillow, and stuff it into the fan of your victim's car. When the car is started, the fan will rip into the pillow, and send up a cloud of downy snow. If you can, use the victim's pillow, or down-filled jacket. Never use your own stuff if you can avoid it. That isn't cost efficient. Always use materials that belong to the victim if you can. It makes them feel much worse.

Drive-up Banking Surprise

There are many reasons to be angry at a bank, from teller abuse, unrecorded deposits, to just plain snotty attitudes. If your bank has one of those drive-up tellers (the kind with the machine that sends your transactions through a tube,) walk up to it, so that you avoid the video camera, and remove the transaction tube. Slightly open a can of carbonated soda pop. Place the can in the tube (if it works without the tube even better,) put it into the proper slot, and push the send button. Inside the bank, the can or tube falls into an open tray, so that the tellers can get to the business at hand. With luck, the can will be shaken up during it's travel into the bank, and spray upwards of ten feet. If the can is still shooting a spray of sticky foam when it arrives, great. If not, you at least know that it gummed up the entire works of the machine.

The tubes are there for your convenience. Use them to unload all sorts of stuff you don't need anymore. Dead (or live) animals, like mice or snakes, or even excrement are a pleasant surprise. Use your imagination. If a teller gives you some shit, return the favor. One guy that I know, spent many days collecting live cockroaches, and used the tube to deliver them right onto the lap of a rude teller. He says that he feels much better. Think of this revenge, then, as a benefit to your mental health.

Drug Store Drama

If you have a good reason to be angry at a drug store, here is a suggestion for revenge. Mix the tubes and boxes of toothpaste and hemorrhoid ointment. Put the toothpaste tubes into the ointment boxes, and vice versa. Chances are, the customer who purchases the mixed up boxes won't notice the mix-up until they're home. You can count on them making a loud and angry report to the management, or even a lawsuit. If by some fluke, they don't notice until it's too late, (say they brush their teeth with hemorrhoid ointment,) maybe their gums will shrink and their teeth will fall out. That's not your problem. It is the store's.

One thing that really bothers pharmacists, is to announce loudly that the "condoms" that you bought there didn't work. Continue to use the pronouncement, "condoms." Condoms this, condoms that. Pharmacists hate the word condoms, so use the word to get their goat. Ask the pharmacist what brand of condoms he or she uses, and which condoms slide in and out the best. Open a package, and unroll one. Wave it around and ask other shoppers which they'd choose for some heavy-duty sex. If you're really a smartass, ask the pharmacist if you can "try this condom on for size."

HEE.
HEE.
HEE.

Drunken Guests

Chances are, if you're the type of person who likes to throw a party once in a while, you'll occasionally end up with a drunken eggs-for-brains idiot who falls asleep on your couch. We all have different ways of dealing with these thoughtless creatures, this is one of my favorites. I take a handful of cigarettes and straws, and poke them gently into the facial holes of the drunken sod. Then I lay women's underware (or vice versa, though there are other things I'd do if there were a drunken lady on my couch) over the person's clothes, so that it looks like he's trying them on. If the person is very drunk and out of it, a few dabs of magenta makeup adds a nice touch to the scenario. After placing an enema bag in the nut's hand, I get out the old 35mm camera, and start snapping. I usually remove all of the stuff and then go to bed. The guy will go home when he wakes up and never know that anything happened . . . until I share the photos with him at a later date.

To the Editor

Sign your victim's name, to an elaborately written letter, speaking out about any inhumane, racist, satanic, dogma that you can think of. Then send the letter to the largest metropolitan newspaper, to the letters section or editor. Keep the letter clean in content, yet praise things like child photography, human sacrifice, blood letting, white supremacy, revolution, etcetera. Give the victim's address, and challenge anyone with opposite views to write and (the victim) will straighten them out. You can start your letter with something like, "Blacks aren't people, really, they're inferior monkeys." That should get your imagination running, and you'll just continue the flow. Use a public typewriter, and the person's stationary if you can get a hold of some.

Exclusive Clubs

If you've been denied access to one of those new nightclubs, where the doorman decides who he'll let in or not, there are a few ways to get even.

One way is to call in a bomb threat. Another is to call the liquor control board, and tell them that you've witnessed them serving minors, more than once. Go ahead and give your name, as the liquor boards keep your reports confidential. You can call the board of health and tell them that you saw a bartender spitting into drinks of people who weren't fashionable enough. Tell the vice squad that the place has house prostitutes, and that you were shocked when they demanded that you pay a prostitute, in order to be allowed entry. If you can afford it, hire prostitutes to work inside the place, tell them that the club owner wanted you to get some girls for the place, and that they have to get naked while dancing or drinking at the bar. Have them strip at an appointed time, then go down on some of the clientel. Be sure to notify the officers of the proper time to arrive, and that the bouncer or doorman is the man in charge of the whores.

Exploding Lamps

If your victim has a wall switch operated lamp, one that turns-on by hitting a switch on the wall, as opposed to the kind that has a switch right on the lamp, take a thin piece of copper wire, and wrap it around the male prongs on the lamp's wall plug. Make sure that the light switch is OFF when you plug the lamp back in, or you'll die. The next time the person enters the room and flips the wall switch, KERDOUGE! Hopefully it'll blow the entire electrical setup in the house. Usually though, the lamp and socket explode in a crackle of smoke and sparks.

Fancy Soaps

If you're in your victim's house using the bathroom, and there are those fancy soaps displayed in a dish, use them. (Most people who keep these little soapy figurines, cherish them.) Use them all, slightly, just enough to ruin each one. Another soap prank is to take a bar of soap, and pop it into the person's microwave, set on high for two minutes. The soap will "cook" until it's melted, and even with a few cleanings, each food dish that's cooked in the microwave will taste and smell of soap.

A Fat Revenge

If your victim is overweight, be sure to sign him up for all of the fat farm, weight loss services. Ask them (in your victim's name) to call you or mail you their information. Tell them that you want copies of their menus, diets, etcetera. Hopefully, they'll contact fatty often, and keep trying to sign him up for their special weight loosing treatments.

If your fat victim is trying to diet seriously, order pizza deliveries, send gourmet magazines to his address, and chocolate bars.

Free Tickets

Call your antagonist, and tell him or her, that they won free tickets to a sold out show. Tell the victim that his name will be on the guest list at the door, and that a table will be reserved, "right up front." Tell him to bring up to six guests, and to show up after eight P.M. Always call the day of the show, and act really excited about being able to make someone so happy.

If it's a rock show, tell the victim that he or she should dress formal. If it's a country show, say that it's "modern dress." Give yourself the opportunity to park nearby, so that you can watch the front door, as your "winner" tries to get in. You can send people to funerals, saying that it's a special costume party, celebrating hedonism, stuff like that.

If you really want to be mean, call the club that you "invited" your victim to. Say that you're the owner of another club, and that (give name of the marked person) has been trying to sneak into your club, by bringing a slew of guests to the door, and claiming that his or her name is on the guest list. They'll be ready for the person with open arms.

Glasses and Contacts

Some pairs of prescription glasses are shaped so that the lenses fit into the opposite holes. Pop out the lenses and switch them.

Another eyeglass prank is to super-glue the frames in the open position. This can be a real pain, you can't put them in a case, or in your pocket. It's a real pain in the glass.

This is a good contact lens gag since most contact lenses are stored in a little device that bathes them, and they are separated so that the wearer doesn't mix them up. Mix them up. Also, a drop or two of ammonia in the rinse mixture causes severe burning. Don't put the ammonia directly into the contact storage container, as the stuff will possibly do permanent damage. Only add a drop or two to the larger eye-rinse bottle. This will dilute it enough to be just an irritant. If ammonia seems a little severe to you, you can always add a few drops of onion juice.

Dramatic Hair Loss in Just a Few Shampoos

Put any of the commercial hair removal products into the person's shampoo bottles. It won't knock out all of the person's hair, but it sure will leave a few bald spots, the size of silver dollars. The victim will look like a refugee from the bowels of Chernobyl.

You can add the same substances to the person's dog shampoo also. They'll think the dog has the mange, and will take it to the vet. The vet's advice will almost certainly be . . . to shampoo the dog more frequently.

You don't necessarily need to enter the person's home to get to the shampoo. If the person goes to a gym, you can open the person's locker and add it there. Another way is to save the small shampoo samples when you get them in the mail. Open the box carefully, add the hair removal product, and reseal. Simply mail the package to the victim, and let the product do the rest.

Don't forget the cream rinse!

Hake Fest

I know a fellow that lives in a small fishing community, just north of San Francisco. He just couldn't handle all of the town's attempts at increasing tourism, by throwing tourist event attractions, at the expense of the locals' privacy. He designed a flier, modeled after the business associations's own promotional posters, and invented a "tourist day" of his own. Since the town already had a "fish fest," a "clam beach run," and five or so other events, my friend decided that his event would show the sponsors the sillyness of their endeavors. The area is known for it's salmon fishing and crabbing, a virtual fisherman's paradise. He called his event, "The Hake Fest." A hake is a type of pacific whiting, a fast rotting, almost worthless bottom fish, that turns to a stinky pudding, only hours after they're caught. The Hake Fest fliers told all visiting fisherman to save their hake, and that there was going to be a judging, a bakeoff, and even a "hake-toss." It would seem that the people who had lived in the town would see the absurdity of the flier, and "get the hint." Not so. Since my friend had taken every precaution to have his flier look like the real thing, some folks fell deeper into his trap than he had planned.

The event's promoters went as far as to take a handful of the Hake Fest fliers into an important town hall meeting, and told the council that "someone is trying to undermine *our* Fish Fest!!" The council discussed the unauthorized event well into the night, and vowed that the Hake Fest wouldn't be allowed to take away from their little tourist fish party. Finally, someone said, "Uh, Mr. Mayor, I'm not sure, but I think that this is a joke." What an ultimate act of revenge, one that just keeps on working for you. Some of the local fishermen have even decided to actually have a Hake Fest, at their nearest opportunity. One fisherman named Skippy, went as far as to claim the Velveeta and hake pizza concession.

Hat Head

Most people who wear hats seldom look inside them before donning them. Coat the entire inside of the victim's hat with petroleum jelly. The person will put on the hat, and wear it while the jelly penetrates the person's hair. When the hat is finally removed, the jelly will have permeated the scalp, and the person's hair will stay in the same shape as it was under the hat, giving them what I call, "hat-head."

Home Delivery and Repair

One time I hated this guy so much, that I devised this little act of revenge. I called up every service orientated company that I could find in the yellow pages, that were in the victim's area. I called a caterer, pizza delivery, the phone company, plumbers, the gas company, exterminaters, construction companys, pool maintenance—you get the idea. I asked them all to arrive at twelve o'clock the following day. I even drove by the deck-head's house at about twelve fifteen. You wouldn't believe the commotion! Trucks and vans were in the street blocking traffic. There were a mess of people with containers and products on the guy's lawn. I could tell that he was going bananas. He was waving his arms and yelling at the people, his face was red and he was drooling as he ranted. The delivery and service people were just as angry at him. It was great.

Homes

Breaking and entering someone's home or automobile is against the law in every state in the union. I don't recommend that you enter anyone's home without permission, but if you do choose to break the law, here are a few nice things that you can do, once inside.

If your enemy has an extensive record collection, take the time to scratch every one of them, with a razor blade or knife. Be sure to replace them all, in their original protective sleeves, so that your victim thinks that all is normal, when the time comes to listen to them. Always begin the scratchings about halfway through the first song, so that the victim hears enough of his favorite music, to begin to enjoy it.

A drop or two of glue, wiped onto the recording heads of tape decks, often sends the tape player into the shop for costly repairs. Better yet, the repair person will probably realize what happened, and will candidly report to the victim, that she or he has been duped.

Look in the bathroom. There is always something useful to a revengster there. Put Tobasco on toothbrushes, in enema bags, or on anal thermometers. This'll show the person that he's hot stuff. If it's a woman's bathroom, garlic salt sanitary pads, or try putting a few drops of yellow and red food coloring on each and every pad. This looks awfully gross, and even the strongest-stomached women would rather use newspaper, than these disgustingly colored stain absorbing devices.

Horned Revenge

Does your enemy have one of those "motion sensitive" auto alarms installed in his car? Be sure to give his front fender a hearty downward shove each and every time you pass the car. Try returning at different times of the day. The victim will begin to receive complaints about the noise, and if he's at work, he'll have to leave often to turn off the sounding horn. You can begin the complaints by calling yourself, saying something like, "Listen buddy, if you don't fix dat horn, I'm gonna call the cops!" Chances are if you do it frequently, the victim will think that the mechanism is broken, and he'll either rip out the wires or take it in to be fixed.

Ink Blots

Buy two of those trick fountain pens that are filled with innocent disappearing ink. Tamper with one of them, and fill it with permanent ink. Carefully reseal the package of the tampered pen. Now go find your victim, and blast the person immediately with the disappearing ink. Explain to the person that it's just a joke, and the ink will soon dissipate. As soon as the stuff disappears, offer the other pen to the victim, telling him that you bought two for the fun of it. It won't be long before the victim takes his shot at someone else. This time, the ink is real, and it'll destroy any clothing it hits. The victim will have to deal with the replacement of the person's clothing, plus the loss of whatever respect the person had for him (if any.)

Keeping Poochie Regular

Has your dog-owning neighbor been letting poochie off his leash at night so that he does his business on your lawn, or empties out your garbage can? Don't get mad at the dog owner. Practice the art of getting even. Take a substantial portion of a potent laxative, and wrap it in a large ball of hamburger meat. Leave the ball of meat near your front porch, and you can bet that poochie will consider it a tasty gift. Later, after Mr. Dog Owner lets poochie in the house for a good night's sleep—well, I'll let you figure it out.

Another special doggie treat, is to wrap four or five Alka-Selzer tablets in hamburger. Poochie will eat the stuff down, but later on, he'll barf a redish, frothy foam. Mr. Dog Owner will think that poochie is rabid, and might even shoot him.

Kitten Helper

If you've been given shoddy treatment at a restaurant, the next time you go in, bring a bag of small, live wildlife in with you. After you're seated comfortably, and your dinner order is in, release the bag of creatures. Use mice, snakes, anything that will scurry away as soon as you let them go. Watch as the things scatter under tables, and into the kitchen. Listen as the other customers begin to see the little buggers. Laugh as the employees run back and forth after the skittling little beasties.

Now, if it's an oriental restaurant, then use kittens. They don't really scurry away as fast as mice, but they'll really give a jolt to someone who is biting into an oriental meat dish, and they hear those sad, lost kitten voices. They might even barf! In fact, if you want to, stick your finger down your throat and make yourself barf. That, along with the mews, should get anyone within smelling distance, to join in the fun.

Lawn Care

If the person who has caused you trouble has a fine green lawn, try this little number. Save all of your old flashlight batteries, in a glass jar filled with water. After a month or so, you'll have a great mixture for "writing" on the person's green. It also works in squirt guns, for use on paint jobs or nylon stockings.

Lesbians

If a haughty lesbian type insists on bothering you, interrupt the conversation, and talk on and on about the Holland dykes. If s/he tries to change the topic, keep reverting back to the Holland dykes, exclaiming how wide they are, and how amazing it is that they retain as much water as they do.

I sometimes like to tell lesbians that we have something in common. I tell them that I'm basically a lesbian in a man's body, with one exception. I tell them that the only difference is that I have a big penis, and they don't. They love that.

Lie Like a Rug

One quick, and very public act of revenge, can be done at any bar or other public arena, and the results are fast and furious. Make up a whopping lie, and tell it "in confidence" to any talkative bartender or waitress. Say something like, "See that mothball over there? That S.O.B. just served a year in prison for cutting the hands off of a neighborhood little girl, after sodomizing her. If you ask me, he should have been hung!" Leave the place quietly, but be sure to leave a large tip, in crisp new dollars. The victim will then be treated with the respect that he deserves.

Get Your Revenge, by Long Distance

In some states this works, and in others it doesn't. You'll have to experiment with it. Say that I'm in someone's house and I want to ring up a big phone bill. I dial a long distance number, say hello, and leave the phone off of the hook. The person that I called can't get a dial tone, and the victim's paying for every minute. Call Mr. Chin in China, or something like that. First call information in China. Ask for the number of Mr. Chin. You're going to get a number.

The Loose Bowel Attack

When somebody you don't like sits in front of you, try this funny revenge. You know how when people sit, there's that small gap between their pants and their body? Break up tiny bits of a chocolate bar, and lightly drop the pieces down that open space. The bits will accumulate in the victim's underware, and will slowly melt from the body heat. When the person gets home and removes the underwear, he or she'll think that they had a back door accident!

The Old Magazine Cover Switcheroo

Buy a brand new porno magazine and carefully remove the cover. Then take a similar size and shaped magazine, remove the cover off of that. Now take the "clean" cover and restaple it to the porno magazine. Leave the clean-covered porno magazine in doctors' offices (if that's who you're mad at) or in a hair salon or laundromat. Since you have the makings of another doctored magazine, place the porno cover on the straight magazine, and sneak it onto the shelves of a store that you hate. Most men who buy mags like Penthouse and Hustler, buy them in grocery stores or convenience stores. They grab their favorite magazine, (with nasty cover) and buy it as quickly as possible.

Your doctored magazine should make it all the way home, and once the person gets it home, he's not likely to return it saying, "Hey! Where's the porn?" The person will probably just steam at home. This is a good one, if you are one of those people who believes that pornography is the devil's photography. I don't need to justify your reasoning for wanting to get even with anyone, it's just a suggestion.

You can do the old magazine switcheroo with Playboy and Playgirl too.

Mailing Labels

Take a bunch of the raunchiest porno magazines that you can find. While you're at it, make sure that you buy some child pornography, and magazines that show beastiality, gay lovers, interracial sexual acts, etc. Anything that you're sure will offend the most seasoned person. Print up some phony mailing labels, complete with the name and address of your enemy.

Stick your lables onto the magazines, and leave the filthy rags all over town. Put them in the person's neighbor's mailbox, at his or her job, even send some to the person's church or social club.

While you have the magazines in your possession, (I'm sure as a connoisseur of fine books like this one, you wouldn't want to read them yourself) get the addresses for the classified sections and send in a few ads for your enemy. Say things like, "I'm into S&M, child bondage, excrement, abuse, etc." Always pay in cash, and be as cruel and nasty as you possibly can. If you have a photo of your victim, send that in too, and ask for companionship, with someone who shares similar tastes. Give the victim's phone number and ask that all responses be called in after twelve midnight, as your working schedule keeps you busy during the day.

Mail-order Brides

This is a good trick to pull on an enemy that is married. Look in the back of almost any magazine, and you'll find those ads that say stuff like, "Foreign marriage-minded girls" or "International directory of marriage-minded men." Sign up your victim, giving the person's phone number and address. As always, pay for the person's enrollment in cash. The victim will begin to receive letters and calls from all corners of the world, asking for marriage. The spouse will walk out after the first few proposals. Be sure to mention that you (the victim) are dissatisfied with your current relationship, and the only way you're going to be happy in life, is to marry a Latin American or Asian person. Whoever writes will probably say in their letters, "Sorry to hear about your unhappy relationship," etcetera.

Make 'Em Wonder

A good way to get even with someone is to make them think that something wierd is going on. Take out a classified ad in a newspaper that you know your victim reads. The ad should say nothing, but the victim's name, in bold letters. Pay for a week's worth of the ad in cash, and give an odd name with payment. Something like Douglas T. Bartlette II, or Rachael Cascade. If this doesn't get the person's mind to wonder, the person probably doesn't have one. If you want to complicate things, instruct the newspaper to remove one letter from the person's name each day. Give an out-of-town address, and then watch the paper!

Minimum Daily Requirement of Vitamins and Insects

There was a great scene in a major horror film, where the guy was infested by a swarm of cockroaches. Try collecting some, as many as you can and filling your victim's cereal boxes, as well as putting them into their can of coffee. If your target has one of those coffee mills, put some roaches in that. The person will grind them up, and enjoy them in a hot drink.

Misc. Auto

Alka-Seltzer tablets crumbled into the water compartments of a car battery renders it useless. The charge will dissipate almost immediately.

As long as you're under the hood, pull out the spark plug wires. Or, if you really want to be nasty, take a pair of locking plyers and bend the tips of the car's fan, so that when the motor is turned over, the blades cut right into the radiator.

Smear petroleum jelly onto the rubber brake pedal of your enemy's car. If lard is available then use that. The slick stuff is hard to remove, if it's even noticed at all. Eventually, a foot is going to slip, and fenders are going to bend. Ahh! Getting even!

If your victim's car is small enough, you should be able to roll it over with the help of a friend or two. This trick almost always ruins the car's paint job, and sometimes breaks out the windows.

It may cost you a few dollars, but if you can't get into your victim's car, then call a locksmith. If he asks you for identification, tell him that you accidentally left it at home. He'll probably believe you, since you already proved that you're slightly incompetent (having lost your car keys.) As soon as the guy leaves, the car is yours to do with what you will.

The Old Beer Blast Maneuver

Find out the address of the person who has done you wrong. Print up a bunch of fliers, which cost only a few dollars per hundred. The fliers should say in bold letters, "Biker's Beer Blast!!" Give the location and address of the lucky host, as well as saying things like, "Free Kentucky whiskey and Buck knives for the first fifty bikers." Spice up the fliers with cutouts from porn and motorcycle magazines, including naked nookies and choppers. Stuff like that.

If you know anything about the area, you can put these things in the ghettos or in sleazy bars, or even advertise in biker's magazines. The response will be unbelievable. Should too many bikers show up and cause great damage to the scumbag who's messed with you, the police will probably arrive in force. Be sure to leave a few at the nearest precinct on the day of the blast. Hopefully, the pissed off bikers will cause structural damage in the surrounding area, and the police will charge the costs to the person who "held the party."

The Parking Violation, Violation

If you happen to notice that your enemy's car has a parking ticket on the windshield, take the ticket. When you get home, take a bold tipped marker and write messages on it. "All cops are homosexual deviants" or "Kill the fascist pig cops" are good enough. Then mail the ticket in to the authorities.

Pencil Pointers

If you drop or tap a pencil on a table, the lead will break up on the inside, while the wood stays intact. Take all of your enemy's pencils, and do this to them. Each time the chump tries to sharpen them, there will never be a tip. This is quite frustrating.

Another fine pencil gimmick: take a pin or needle, and break off the sharp end with two pairs of plyers. Pop out the eraser from the victim's pencil, and bury the shortened pin into the eraser until just the pointy tip comes up through the eraser. Then replace the eraser so that the pin point is barely visible. When the victim tries to erase a mistake, the pin will tear into the page, and ruin it.

Phone Busters

Unplug the enemy's phone jack from the wall. Coat the end of the connection with epoxy or glue and then replace it. Repeat the process with the jack that plugs into the phone. The victim will be certain that the problem lies in the phone itself, and will probably replace it.

Phone Sex

If the person you hate is an employee where you work, and you have access to his or her phone, make calls to the 900 porn lines whenever possible. When the boss gets the phone bill, your victim will have hell to pay, trying to get out of that one.

If you can do this at the person's home and he or she is married, so much the better. The phone numbers usually have creative numbers, like "900-SEX-SLAV" or things like that. Call whenever you can, and keep the calls lengthy.

These services sometimes offer call-backs, so be sure to have them call back around dinner time. Mention that it would be more pleasurable for you if they said something really dirty when you answer the phone.

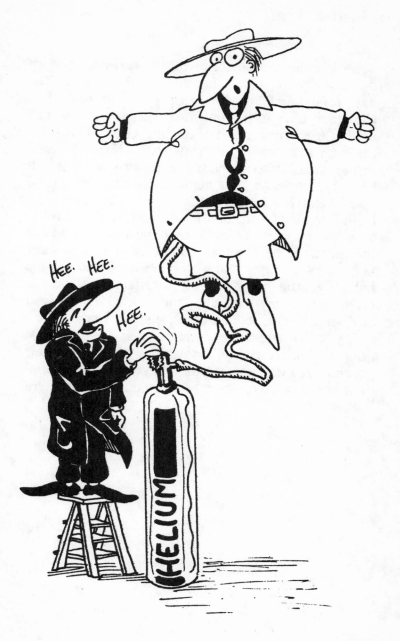

Plant a Tree

Besides his new theories of our understanding of the atom, G.N. tells this tale of reforestation. The days following Christmas, people tend to leave their Christmas trees in front of their houses, to be picked up by the sanitation department. G.N. drives his truck up and down the streets, collecting these discarded trees. After gathering as many trees that will fit in his truck, he goes home and waits for night to fall. Then around three in the morning, he takes them to the home of someone he dislikes, and "plants" them in the yard. When the victim looks outside in the morning, he's got an entire forest in the yard. G.N. says that this prank isn't reserved just for the holiday season. He says that on certain days, he can drive through any large city, and pick up a truck load of discarded chairs, mattresses, old bed frames, etc.

If you live where the street pickings are poor, just offer to collect people's trash, or clean out their garages. In a day's work you'll have enough material to make any lawn look like an outdoor furniture warehouse.

I Pledge Allegiance, to Revenge . . .

Always call in and pledge large amounts of money in your enemy's name, during fundraising telethons. A simple way to do this is to say that you'll donate a thousand dollars to the needy organization, only if they say your (the victim's) name, business name, and location on the air. If your enemy is the boss of a certain type of business, have the announcers challenge the competition on the air. Another sure fire way to practically force the victim to pay, is to say that he or she is making this generous donation, "in the name of my loving mother." Whether the person pays or not, they'll feel real bad, every time they get those notices that their pledge is due to be paid. Chances are, the person will find out about it whether or not they saw or heard their name on the air. Employees will compliment them on their generosity, making it very difficult not to pay up.

Poison Oaf

Most drug stores sell small bottles of extract of poison oak. These can be used in lots of ways. You can pour it into liquid laundry soap, or directly onto clothing. You can line the rim of a drinking glass with it, leaving an interesting trail of raw pimple-flesh on the person's lips. You can an put it into shampoo bottles, or hair tonic. It will easily mix with body oils, or massage lotion. Buy the stuff in bulk, and ponder the many possibilities.

Poison Pretties

Always send large bouquets of expensive flowers to the person who has wronged you. Long stemmed red roses, look beautiful when set in a splay of poison oak, or poison ivy. This assortment is as huggable as a spring lamb, and whoever receives the gift will sing your praises for hours. They can be sent to beauty pageants, hospitals, or to someone's office. Give the gift of poison ivy.

HEE.
HEE.

SLAM!

The Popcorn Presentation

My brother had this sales job. He had a very important presentation to make, and I was angry with him. I filled his briefcase full of popcorn. When it came time to give his presentation, he had nothing but popcorn. Come to think of it, I haven't really seen him since.

Potato as Projectile

I'm sure you've heard of this one before, but I can't help but remind you of it. It's so simple, yet it is a powerful reminder of the simplicity of a classic revenge. Cram a potato into the exhaust pipe of the victim's car. When the unsuspecting crumb starts the car, the pressure will build to such an extent that the spud blows out of the tail pipe with enough force to penetrate a wooden garage door. Or better yet, if there is another car parked behind it, it might even hit a windshield or headlight.

Powered by Pudding

Pour a box or two of instant pudding into the gas tank of your victim's car. If you really want to have the stuff become pudding, pour it into the radiator or use it as an oil additive.

Pray for Revenge

This method hasn't worked for me. I suggest that you take a more direct approach.

Public Restroom Enemy Number One

The public restroom may seem to have a shortage of revengeful pranks available. Not so. There are just as many things you can do in one as there are in people's homes. This one is kind of gross, so bear with me. Usually, a screwdriver or hair pin will unlock the soap fixtures in public restrooms. Remove the top of the liquid soap dispenser, and urinate in it. Then crap in the sink. Then ball up as many wads of paper towels as you feel necessary, and jam them down the commode. Turn off all water by using the little knobs under the sink. Remove all of the light bulbs or tubes. Flush the toilet and leave.

Here's a good one for ladies' rooms. Pick up a few free bumper stickers from the local blood bank, the ones that say things like, "Give the gift of blood." Stick these on the containers made for disposing sanitary napkins and tampons. If it's a relatively classy establishment, expect complaints.

Another sticker idea that can be used in restrooms is to take the stickers off of the counters of convenience stores that say, "closed circuit camera in operation." Put these in the stalls, or onto the mirrors.

The Revenge Cookie

Two guys who I'll call D.B. and R.V. (even though their real names are David Brattstrom and Steve Vidovich) cooked up a batch of revenge cookies that you wouldn't believe. These two cranksters had a disagreement with the swim team of their school's P.E. department. They whipped up a batch of chocolate chip cookies, and instead of using chocolate, they chipped up a package of a popular chocolate laxative. When the cookies were done, they looked just like the kind mom used to make. They even appeared to taste as good, too, as the entire swim team ate them gleefully at a party, the night before a big swim meet. One character kept coming back for more. Since D.B. and S.V. had figured that two cookies maximum, could safely be eaten per person, they said no. The guy didn't heed their warning, though, and ate more than his share. D.B. laughs as he recalls how the girls would swim a race, then leap out of the pool and run into the bathroom, then they'd run (bad choice of words) back to the pool to swim again. Then they'd repeat the procedure. This one is not for the weak-hearted.

The Revengefull Turn-On

Turning everything on, can make the victim feel violated. Turn on everything in the person's home. The heater, the oven and stove, TV, stereo, lights, water, fans, blenders, coffee pot, microwave (set at ten hours on low,) and any other thing that you can find that has a switch.

In the auto, do the same thing, only exclude the lights. If they are on, the battery might drain and the gag wouldn't work. Turn on the wipers, the radio (as loud as it will go,) the heater and all blowers, air conditioning, etc.

A Runny Mocha Treat

B.D. of California, has this recipe for chocolate coated asshole. She suggests that you place a chocolate candy bar atop an overhead light. Soon after your victim turns on the lighting, and settles down to work, the thing will start to melt all over the person. If the lighting covers a large area, I recommend that you use more than one chocolate bar.

Scare the Salesman

If you are bothered by a pesty overeager salesman, and you realize that he's not going to leave until a sale is made, try this. Ask the salesman in, and tell him to sit down. Tell him that you have just a few things to do before he begins, and that you'd appreciate it if he'd sit down and prepare his presentation while you take care of them. Assure him that you'll be back in just a few moments, but that you'd appreciate it if he'd answer the phone for you if it rings.

Now leave out of the back door, and go to a previously agreed with neighbor, a very big male, and tell him that a pushy salesman is at your home. Have the neighbor call your house, and when the salesman answers the phone, have him scream in a seemingly jealous, drunken state. "I'm coming over in one minute, and you better be gone, and that bitch better be ready for some heavy fornicating!" (Gotta keep it clean, this is a classy book.) Next, the neighbor should arrive at the back door before the salesman has time to gather his demo materials, or his thoughts. Have the neighbor pound loudly, so that the whole house shakes, while calling out your name. This is when you come back, to the front door, looking worried and frightened for the salesman's life. Tell him that "Bruno" raped the last salesman who he caught with her. The demonstration should be over at this point, and the salesman should be long gone.

Invite Bruno in for a drink.

Screw Happy

With a screwdriver (see "Tools of the Tirade") remove each and every magnet or clip from all of the cupboards, closets, and shower stall door of your enemy's house. This is frustrating and time consuming for the victim, and makes you feel much better.

While you are in the cupboards, use your screwdriver to scratch up all nonstick surfaced cookware, and punch holes in all of the food containers.

A Shocking Revelation

If the person you hate works for a company that functions amid fierce competition, call the person's boss, and say that you work for the competition. Tell the victim's boss that he or she had filled out an application for employment, and you are just checking on the person's references and qualifications. For instance, if the person works for Coca-Cola, call up and say that you are in charge of hiring for Pepsi. The call might lose the person his job, but you can be certain that it will at least make things more difficult for the person, and you can bet the boss will have second thoughts about giving him a raise.

Sick and Tired

If the person who has done you wrong has a job, help that person to lose it. About an hour before the victim is due to show up at work, call him up and pretend that you are his (or her, you feminist paranoids) boss, and that you've been cutting back on the work force. Say that you decided to cut the most unproductive workers first, and that (s)he was at the top of the list. Tell the person to come in at the usual time, only to pick up a paycheck instead of going to work. Hang up. Now, call in for the person, ask for the boss, and act like the person you want fired. Slur your words, as though you're a little drunk, and tell the boss that you're too sick to come to work. "In fact," you say rudely, "I'm sick all right. I'm sick and tired! I wouldn't work for you any more if you paid me!" Be sure to rant like you're high on anger, then demand that your check be ready for you when you come in to work. Call the boss a filthy name, or comment on his or her sexual abilities, and hang up. Chances are, few words will be exchanged when the victim arrives, and the boss will probably refuse to talk to him. The chump will pick up his check and storm out the door, quite possibly thinking about going to the labor board, or a lawyer.

93

Signs for the Times
(when you've had it up till now)

Steal real estate signs from various homes or apartments. Late at night sneak them into your enemy's lawn and shove their stakes into the ground. One clever guy I know found over a hundred real estate signs in one night, and with his help, they all made their way onto the lawn of a local schmidiot.

If you don't feel like stealing, (very commendable of you,) take the time to make your own signs. They should say things like: "God loves homosexuals," "I support the KKK-up with white supremacy," "AIDS testing," "Drive through abortion clinic," "F*ck America." Another good message is "Child molester." Nobody likes a child molester, and your victim can swear innocence all he or she wants to. Secretly, people will always remember reading that sign.

Special Gift

Take a nice gift box and put in some soft packing material. Then place a high priced price tag, from the most exclusive, expensive store available to you. Without putting anything else in the gift box, wrap it in lavish wrapping paper topped with a bow, and deliver it to your enemy. When he or she opens the box, and looks through the wrapping material for the "gift," all that will be found is the expensive tag. The victim will be in a tizzy trying to figure out what to do. He can't call you and say, "Hey, you forgot the gift!" All he can do is look at the expensive price tag, and wonder what he didn't get.

Star Struck

On your victim's stationary, write dirty fan letters to famous stars, inviting them to engage in sodomy or beastiality. Sign your victim's name and address, and add in the postscript that you plan to seek out the performer and force him or her into the acts at the nearest opportunity.

Get the phone numbers of the star's agent or network affiliate, and call frequently, asking for the star while you pretend to masturbate. The next time the star visits the mark's hometown, you can bet he'll be visited by the star's personal associates, or even the police.

Stereo Drama

Always turn up the volume to it's highest point, when you see that your victim has an expensive stereo system. You should do this when the stereo is turned off, of course. The next time the chump flips on the radio or plays a new C.D., the speakers should blow out. That will teach 'em.

Stinky, Stanky & Sticky

Automobiles are a fine target for revenge. They are expensive, almost everyone owns one, and they are extremely costly to fix. There are hundreds of dirty things that can be done to automobiles, from scratching the paint to blowing them up. If the schmeghead has taken it upon himself to screw you over, get your revenge through his favorite possession—his automobile.

An open, thawed can of concentrated orange juice makes for a creamy, sticky auto seat covering. If you take a can of it while it is still frozen, open the can and put it in the victim's glove compartment. When the goop thaws, it'll ruin everything in the glove compartment. Use two cans if you feel like it. If your enemy's been lying to you, use this method to make the person "stick" to his word.

Larry, the Walla Walla Worm Wrangler suggests that you take two or three dead fish, and place them into a bucket of water. Let the fish soak in the water for a good five days in a warm environment. The water should take on all the qualities of the rotting fish, namely the stench. After curing the fish for an extended amount of time, throw them out, but save the water. Take this fishishly designed water, and pour it onto the carpets of your enemy's car. The stench will be almost impossible to remove. Several cleanings are required, yet the stank still lingers, if you aged the fish properly.

The W.W.W. Wrangler also suggests that you take a small fish, a herring or sardine, and tuck it up into the heating coil of your victim's car heater. Substitute dung for fish if you want.

T-Square = Revenge^2

Here is one way to get even with a graphic artist. Empty out the artist's pencil sharpener, and glue the shavings to the bottom of the surface of the person's T-square. Most of the graphite will be exposed, and even the slightest artistic adjustment, will ruin at least one work of art. Nothing makes artists madder, than ruining their own work.

Tear Gas Treat

As almost any housewife can tell you, it takes a gas mask to breathe if you've accidentally mixed amonia and bleach. Take equal parts amonia and bleach then, and mix them in a cleaning bottle with a spray nozzle. Take the bottle to any public place and begin squirting. Pretty soon you'll see people rubbing their eyes as the tears start to flow. In closer quarters, the stuff really has a strong effect.

Those Parking Fools

Are you tired of those idiots who snuggle right up to your bumper and literally pin you into your parking space? You know the type. They get so close that a cat couldn't walk between the two cars. If that happens to you, you don't have to wait, or make a thirty point turn to escape. Slowly inch your car forward until you make contact with the offending vehicle. When you have a solid connection, quickly stomp on the gas and then stomp on the brake.

The force of your shortstop acceleration should do one of two things.

1. Since most people park with their wheels turned toward the curb, the car should leap onto the curb. It might even take out a parking meter, and we can do with less of those anyway.

2. If the wheels are turned into the street, the car will end up in the street.

I've done this little act of reciprocation in quiet neighborhoods and on city streets. One car I did this to happened to be in forward gear, and when I gave it the fatal push, it almost started up! I left it sideways in the southbound lane as I roared around it screaming, "Where'd you learn to park, Chinatown?!" out of my window.

Should the car's wheels be pointing straight ahead, gently push the thing into a red zone. Don't worry about whether or not the car's emergency brake is on. If it is on, you'll probably strip it. The power from your vehicle should override most brakes.

If by chance the car damages a car in front of it when you shove it forward, drive on and park about a block away. Walk back to the vehicle and leave a note on the windshield of the innocent vehicle, that

says something like, "The car behind you came roaring into the parking place and hit your car. He seemed drunk, and left the scene without bothering to look at the damage. Signed, a concerned citizen." Don't forget to jot down the license number on the note, in case the car leaves.

Tools of the Tirade

Battery powered tools are THE revengster's best asset. A battery operated screwdriver can be set on reverse and will quickly and quietly remove screws from door handles, door hinges, water faucets, car door panels, and car mirrors. Snap on a socket adapter, and you can remove the bolts which hold down toilets, light fixtures, lug nuts, etcetera. These screwdrivers can be purchased for under twenty dollars, and they are made by the best manufacturers of power tools.

Battery powered drills and jigsaws are also useful, so buy an assortment, and get even.

Top That!

Bottle cappers are cheap and easy to use. Buy one that is small enough to be easily hidden. Some of them are three feet high, and have huge wooden handles. These are too big. Get the kind that fits in your pocket. They're selling for around five dollars.

Sneak into your enemy's soda or beer supply, pop the tops off, and fill them with whatever you prefer. If it's a few bottles of beer, substitute the liquid with urine. If it's dark enough to hide solid objects, then you can add marbles, worms, or dead insects. Snakes are small enough to slide into a bottle, and so are rabbit pellets. Whatever you decide is best for your particular victim is what works best. Replace the tampered bottles (recapped) in the victim's refrigerator, cupboards, or if the person owns one, on the shelves of his store. Top that!

Towing the Line

Have you ever seen parked cars being towed away by the sanitation department? Well, when the sanitation department is going to tow away an abandoned car, they put these orange stickers on them, and they write a code number on the windshield with a permanent, fat-tipped black marking pen.

If you know where your enemy parks, take the sticker off of an abandoned car, marked for towing by the sanitation department. Put the sticker on your enemy's car, then write the same code number on the windshield. Take off the license plates, and they'll take away the car! After I do this to someone who has really deserved it, I like to get in my own car, and take a nice leisurely drive. The world seems like a better place.

Traitor!

Accuse your victim of selling secrets to the Soviet Union, or any other "enemy." Take photo-copies of technical information that you can find in the library, and stamp the copies with rubber stamps that you have already had made up, (they cost only a couple of dollars to have made up) saying, "Top Secret" or "National Security, Top Priority." Send these to the Russian Embassy, to places like Iran (where you know the U.S. C.I.A. types will open it and read the contents.) Along with your "secrets," send a typewritten letter (use a public library's typewriter or one in a copy store) asking for $10,000 and asylum. Tell them that you (the victim) want to defect, and that nothing American is sacred to you. Finish the letter up with something like, "I have lived in this rotten country long enough, it's time for a change. Long live Stalin!" You can send a duplicate letter to the C.I.A., the F.B.I., the White House, etc. Be careful, these guys are pretty sharp, and if you're the least bit sloppy, they'll find out that it was you who wrote the letter, after they've harrassed the victim, of course.

Transvestite Hookers

You've heard the one about sending a transvestite hooker to your enemy's address, right? Well here's a twist to that classic. A lot of those sex newspapers carry these ads for transvestites that will come to your house. Instead of sending them to the victim's house, send them to the stuffiest neighbor's house in the guy's neighborhood. Send them to the local priest's place, or some other straight type. Think of what (that will do,) when a transvestite hooker shows up at the highbrow neighbor's house looking for the victim, by name! If there are no transvestites available, try overweight black hookers or one of those leatherette sweethearts, that arrive wearing leather bras and carrying whips.

Tubular!

With a ten dollar hand-operated tire pump, blow up the victim's bicycle tires just to the point of intensity. When the victim climbs aboard to ride, BLAM! The tires will blow out. Another tire tube trick, which takes a little longer to do, really drives 'em nuts. Take the person's tire, let out the air and remove the tube. With a razor blade or scissors, cut a large hole in the tube. Make it big enough to fit a hand full of bottlecaps and stones. Take a tire patch kit, and repair the hole. Replace the tire on the bike after the patch sets. The rider will go nuts trying to find out what's going on. The bike will sound like a broken piece of junk.

Typewriters

A small metal file can remove the die of the part that stamps onto the paper. The victim will sit down to type, and nothing but blats and blotches will appear on the page. This ruins the typewriter for good, so take caution when doing this to someone's typewriter.

Vibrators

Let's assume that you have found yourself in the bedroom of the person who's done you wrong, and you've come across the person's vibrator. Take out the batteries, and replace them with batteries that have just a little charge left in them. If you don't have almost-dead batteries, then simply take out the ones in the vibrator. You can just imagine your enemy pulling out the vibrator, ready for an erotic, humming treat, only to hold a motionless tool. If you are able to replace them with batteries that are almost-dead, they should run out of power, halfway into the person's activities. It might as well be a banana. Oh well, life is full of disappointments.

A drop or two of hot sauce smeared over the thing should spice up the person's sex life. Try doing this, for a modern version of the hot-foot.

Video Tape Snip-Snap

If your victim has an extensive collection of video tapes, take them one by one and get your revenge through them. Simply lift the black plastic bar which protects the actual tape portion of the cassette. Cut the tape with a pair of scissors, then move on to the others. This works great with rented tapes too.

Of course if you don't want to go to all that trouble, you can also just run a strong magnet over the tapes. That will erase the recorded images.

Wanted, Dead or Alive.

Steal a really raunchy wanted poster from a post office. Get one that has all sorts of cruel and vicious deeds accredited to the wanted person. Take a picture of the person that you want to get even with, and glue it over the original face. Any typesetter will type up the victim's name in a nice bold typeface for a couple of dollars. Have one typeset your victim's name, and glue that to the poster too, covering the original name. Then take your wanted poster to a photocopy center, and print up as many of the things as you can afford. Post them late at night all over town, on bulletin boards, store windows, telephone poles, etcetera. If you can find an original wanted poster with deeds such as child kidnapping, rape, sodomy, or evil stuff like that, all the more better.

Wax Ashtrays

Coat the inside bottom of the victim's ashtrays with melted wax. With a soft cloth, rub the wax into the ashtray so that it is unnoticable. As soon as the target sits a cigarette into the ashtray, the remaining wax will begin to stink and the cig will be unsmokable.

Whoop!

With a socket set, remove the bolts that hold the seat part of a toilet seat down. Then lay the loose seat back onto the toilet so it appears to still be fastened. As soon as your dupe sits down to take a number two, Whoop! The seat will slide out from under them, and send them onto the floor. It is even possible that during the frightening fall from the commode, the person will be forced to continue his business he started when he originally sat down.

Wire Cutters

A small pair of wire cutters can do many useful, revengeful acts, all in the privacy of your enemy's home. Pull out all electric cords from your enemy's appliances, then take the trusty wire cutters, and clip off just one of the male prongs. Do this to every single appliance that the victim owns, then plug them all back into the wall. The cords will still be plugged in, yet none of them will work. While you're at it, clip off the heating coils of the oven or stove, cut the curtain cords, toilet chains, and phone lines.

It's a Wrap!

Let's say you really want to get even with a woman. Take a roll of cellophane kitchen food-wrap, and sneak into the woman's bathroom with it, and tear off a sheet that is just big enough to cover the toilet bowl. Lift up the seats, and cover the ceramic rim of the bowl with the cellophane. Spread it tight so that it covers the entire opening, and doesn't show any creases or folds. Now put the lids back down, unscrew the lightbulb, and leave quietly. The next time she goes in to relieve herself, she'll think that she just sat down in a rain forest. This works well in public restrooms too, but try not to do this to an innocent woman. It can ruin their whole day.

Yuck!!

This one is called Yuck!! for a reason. It is so gross that I'd have a hard time getting it down on paper, if it wasn't so darn funny. Take a pack of condoms, and open as many of them as your victim has doors in his or her house or office. Let's say that the victim has two doors for the benefit of expediency. Open two condom foil-wrapped packages and unroll the rubbers. Squirt a healthy portion of dish washing liquid into them. (Some people use the white liquid, I prefer the kind that is slightly yellow.) Now spread the rubber's opening so that it is wide enough to fit over a door knob. Put the two filled condoms onto the victim's doorknobs, so that the person will have a hard time getting them off. The looks on people's faces, when they come across these disgusting little presents is priceless. In one way or another, the victim is going to have to remove the things in order to enter the building. Whether they use their hands or some kind of tool, they are going to be forced to remove the rubbers themselves. Yuck!!

Final Note

Well I hope that you've enjoyed this little compendium of tactical revenge. Use the methods shown, to make your unique style of revenge the best that it can be. It's time you and I get down to serious business, and take care of ourselves. Getting even isn't being cruel or vicious. It is an art. When you've begun to master the art of getting even, you'll see that there is no better way to gain restitution from the steaming idiots of the world. Give 'em hell.